The Devil's Label

Who Told You That's Who You Are?

Prophetess Dr. Racheal Odoy

A journey of identity, healing, and truth, exposing the quiet lies that shape who we become.

Copyright 2026 Prophetess Dr. Racheal Odoy

Giant Publishing Company
Post Office Box 6455
Lincoln, NE 68506
www.giantpublishingcompany.com

Printed in the United States of America.

All rights reserved. No part of this publication may be used or reproduced in any form or by any means, electronic or mechanical, including photocopying, recording, or by any information storage and retrieval system, without prior written permission from the author, except for brief quotations used in reviews or articles.

Scripture quotations are from the King James Version (KJV) of the Holy Bible unless otherwise specified. Scripture references, where used, are for inspirational and educational purposes.

ISBN: 979-8-9898098-6-8
Odoy, Racheal

The Devil's Label

Non-fiction/Racheal Odoy

1. Non-fiction - Christianity
2. Christian living
3. Self-help

Cover design: Prophetess Dr. Racheal Odoy

This book is a work of inspirational nonfiction. While it draws from real-life experiences, names, identifying details, and circumstances have been changed where necessary to protect privacy. Any resemblance to actual persons, living or deceased, is coincidental.

Also by Prophetess Dr. Racheal Odoy:

You Need a Jonathan
Copyright 2018

I and My Seed will Thrive
Copyright 2019

You Have No Carbon Copy
Copyright 2020

Arise, Woman of Light
Copyright 2025

The Kiss of Death
Copyright 2025

The Power of the Mirror
Copyright 2026

DEDICATION

This book is dedicated to those who were called something they were never created to be. It is for the ones who carried labels that bruised the soul, yet never erased the truth placed within them by God. It is for those who tried to live up to names they did not choose, and for those who quietly wondered if they would ever be seen beyond what happened to them.

It is also dedicated to those who have always chosen to see people beyond the label. To the ones who looked past appearances, past history, and past mistakes, and instead saw value, potential, and dignity. To those who embraced the broken without judgment, stood beside the wounded with patience, and supported the journey of healing with love, truth, and compassion.

May these pages honor both the ones who were hurt and the ones who helped them heal. And may every reader be reminded that identity is not defined by labels, but by truth—and truth has the power to restore what was almost lost.

ACKNOWLEDGEMENT

I begin with gratitude to God, whose truth restores what lies attempt to distort. This book exists because of His patience, His mercy, and His unwavering commitment to reveal identity beyond circumstance. In moments of silence, questioning, and obedience, He remained faithful to remind me that truth still speaks louder than deception.

I am deeply grateful to my husband, whose support, strength, and understanding have been a constant covering throughout this journey. Your encouragement, prayers, and steady presence have given me room to write, to reflect, and to remain anchored. This work carries the quiet evidence of your partnership and belief in the assignment entrusted to me.

To my children, thank you for being my daily reminder of purpose, resilience, and love. You are my joy, my motivation, and my living testimony that identity is formed in truth, nurtured in love, and protected through presence. Your patience and grace have made this journey possible in more ways than you know.

I also extend my sincere gratitude to every person who trusted me with their story, their pain, and their process of healing. Your courage to confront labels and pursue truth has shaped the heart of this book. To those who walk alongside others with compassion, wisdom, and understanding your quiet labor matters more than words can express.

Finally, to the reader holding this book, thank you for being willing to look inward with honesty and courage. May these pages serve as a safe place to question what you were told, rediscover who you are, and walk forward unburdened by labels that were never yours to carry.

INTRODUCTION

At some point in life, most people stop asking who they are and begin living according to what they were told. Words spoken in childhood, moments of trauma, repeated failures, cultural expectations, and even well-intended opinions slowly shape an identity that may never have been true to begin with. Over time, these words settle into the heart and begin to function as truth—quietly directing decisions, relationships, confidence, and self-worth.

This book was written for those moments when something inside you whispers, *This cannot be all that I am*.

Labels are powerful. They simplify people, reduce complexity, and assign meaning without understanding context. Some labels are spoken by others, while some are formed through painful experiences. Many are reinforced by repetition until they feel permanent. Yet not every name given to you was meant to define you, and not every identity you learned was yours to keep.

As a minister, counselor, and observer of human behavior, I have seen how deeply labels wound how they follow people into adulthood, influence choices, and quietly govern lives. I have also witnessed how healing begins when a person dares to question the label rather than accept it. Freedom often starts with a single, honest question: *Who told me this is who I am?*

This book is not written to condemn, accuse, or reopen wounds without purpose. It is written to invite reflection, truth, and restoration. It is for those who have felt unseen, misnamed, misunderstood, or confined by an identity shaped through pain rather than truth. It is also for those who desire to understand others more deeply and learn how to see beyond appearances and assumptions.

You will not be asked to deny what happened to you. Experiences matter. Pain matters. But experiences are not identities, and pain does not have the authority to rename you. Healing begins when truth is allowed to speak louder than memory, shame, or fear.

Before we begin this journey, pause for a moment. Allow yourself to be honest. Allow yourself to feel. The pages ahead are not meant to rush you, but to walk with you as you begin separating who you are from what you were called.

The poem that follows gives voice to what many carry silently. Let it speak where words have been difficult to find. Let it prepare your heart for the question that will open this book and perhaps change how you see yourself.

THE LABEL

I have tried to fit in places
some welcomed me,
others rejected me
before they ever knew my name.
Because of my label.
Like the tag on a shirt,
I was inspected,
measured,
then quietly discarded
cut off and thrown away
when I didn't meet the standard.
I tried to stand,
but my label made demands of me.
It told me how to behave,
what to expect,
how little I was allowed to hope.
It started claiming my identity
the moment I tried it on.
And now, it will not let me go.
I ask myself questions
I do not know how to answer:
Who am I?
What happened to me?
Why do I hate myself
for wounds I did not choose?
I am lost.
I am lonely.
I am hungry for truth
and cold from the absence of love.

I cannot think clearly anymore
the label shouts louder
than my own voice.
Who can I talk to?
Who would even understand?
Everyone around me looks so complete,
so polished,
so certain of who they are.
And every eye I meet
feels like judgment.
So I cry for help
because I am helpless
not broken,
just buried under a name
that was never mine.
Look at me.
Not for what I was called
but for who I am.
Help me cut off the label
so I can awaken.

TABLE OF CONTENTS
Title Page
Copyright
Dedication
Acknowledgement
Introduction
The Label *(Poem)*

Chapter One	**Page**
Who Told You That?	1

– The day a name entered your story
– When the label stops being outside you
– The enemy's old strategy: distort identity first
– The woman reduced to her worst moment
– Rahab: When faith breaks the label
– Why labels feel impossible to remove
– The question that breaks the agreement
– Reflection

Chapter Two
How Labels Are Formed   9

– Labels are not born; they are learned
– The power of words spoken over time
– When pain explains what words did not say
– Hagar: labeled, forgotten, yet seen by God
– Repetition turns labels into agreements
– Jacob: when a name shapes a life
– Why awareness is the first step to freedom

Chapter Three
When Labels Are Reinforced by Religion, Culture, and Comparison   15

– When systems strengthen the label
– When religion shifts from healing to measuring

– The Pharisees: correct in doctrine, blind in identity
– Culture and the quiet pressure to perform
– Comparison: the thief that looks harmless
– Mary and Martha: when comparison distorts worth
– When labels feel spiritually justified
– Reflection

Chapter Four   **Page**
Living Under a Label You Did Not Choose   **21**
– When identity is shaped without consent
– The subtle cost of adaptation
– Moses: labeled by fear before he was called by God
– When the label becomes a boundary
– Gideon: called while still hiding
– The fear of living without the label
– Reflection

Chapter Five
Breaking the Agreement With the Label   **27**
– Freedom begins where agreement ends
– The inner "yes" that sustains the label
– Why letting go feels like losing control
– Peter: when a label is spoken by Jesus Himself
– Replacing the label requires more than awareness
– When truth feels unfamiliar
– The courage to say no internally
– Reflection

Chapter Six
Who You Are Beneath the Label   **33**
– Identity exists before the label falls away

– The false fear of becoming nothing
– David: anointed before he was acknowledged
– What remains when the label is challenged
– When truth feels like exposure
– Jesus and the question of identity
– Learning to live from the inside out
– Reflection

Chapter Seven — Page
When God Calls You by a Different Name — 39
– Names carry authority
– Abram to Abraham: when promise interrupts limitation
– Why God renames before we are ready
– Simon to Peter: when instability meets calling
– When the old name tries to follow you
– Saul to Paul: when purpose redefines identity
– Learning to answer to the new name
– When God's name conflicts with your feelings
– Reflection

Chapter Eight
Healing the Wounds That Gave the Label Power — 45
– Labels draw strength from unhealed pain
– Why avoided pain continues to speak
– The difference between remembering and reliving
– The woman with the issue of blood: a wound carried for years
– Why healing often feels slower than deliverance
– When healing threatens the label
– Healing reclaims authority from the past
– Reflection

Chapter Nine	**Page**
Learning to See Yourself Clearly Again	51

– When distortion becomes familiar
– The mirror we learn to use
– Why clear vision feels uncomfortable at first
– Blind Bartimaeus: when vision is restored, identity changes
– Separating observation from judgment
– When old images try to resurface
– Seeing yourself as God sees you
– Clarity restores dignity
– Reflection

Chapter Ten
Living Free Without Needing the Label   57

– Freedom is not the absence of memory
– When the label is no longer needed
– Freedom requires responsibility
– Joseph: free before the circumstances changed
– Living without needing to be understood
– The return of simplicity
– When the old voice tries to return
– Living forward without negotiation
– Reflection

Final Chapter
Who Told You the Truth About You?   61

– The most important voice was always the last one
– Who told you the truth about you?
– Truth was present before the label ever arrived
– When Jesus spoke, identity was restored
– Truth does not compete – it replaces
– Living answered instead of questioning
– The quiet authority of knowing who you are

– When the old label no longer answers you
– You were always more than the name you were given
– Reflection
Prayer
Author's Note
About the Author

CHAPTER ONE
Who Told You That?

The Day a Name Entered Your Story
No one is born already reduced to a single word. A child does not arrive in the world convinced she is "too much," or "not enough," or "unwanted." A boy does not enter life believing he is a mistake, a disappointment, or a burden. Those are learned conclusions. They are not birthmarks; they are messages. They are not identity; they are interpretation.

At some point, a name entered your story. Sometimes it entered through a parent's frustration, spoken in a moment they never thought would matter. Sometimes it came from a teacher, a friend, a sibling, a spouse, a leader, or a crowd. Sometimes it came through an experience - abandonment, abuse, betrayal, poverty, failure, rejection - something so painful that it felt easier to accept a label than to keep standing in the mystery of why it happened. And sometimes, the label did not come from what someone said. It came from what someone repeatedly did.

Neglect can label you as "unimportant." Abuse can label you as "worthless." Silence can label you as "invisible." Rejection can label you as "unlovable."

Most labels do not begin as identity. They begin as a suggestion. But when a suggestion is repeated long enough, it becomes a belief. And when a belief is carried long enough, it becomes a lens. This is how a label becomes a life.

When the Label Stops Being Outside You
There is a moment when labels stop sounding like other people and start sounding like you. At first, you hear them externally spoken in a voice, expressed through an action, implied by a look. But over time, labels settle into the heart and begin speaking from within.

That is why labels are so dangerous. They do not merely describe; they direct. They influence what you attempt, what you avoid, what you tolerate, what you expect, and what you believe you deserve. They control what you call "normal." They shape the kind of love you accept. They determine the level of respect you feel entitled to receive. They can even shape the kind of God you believe in because when someone feels unworthy, they often assume God must feel the same way. Scripture speaks to this hidden power of internal belief: *"For as he thinketh in his heart, so is he."* **Proverbs 23:7**

Your thinking becomes your posture. Your posture becomes your choices. Your choices become your patterns. And your patterns, over time, begin to look like your identity.

Yet a pattern is not identity. A label is not truth. And a voice is not authority just because it was loud, early, or repeated.

The Enemy's Old Strategy: Distort Identity First
The enemy's strategy has always been to attack identity before purpose. When a person knows who they are, they become difficult to manipulate. When a person is stable in truth, they become difficult to intimidate. But when identity is confused, the enemy does not need to stop you—he only needs to steer you. This is why the first conflict in the garden was not simply about fruit. It was about identity and truth. The temptation began with a question that targeted certainty: *"Yea, hath God said…?"* **Genesis 3:1**

Once truth is questioned, identity becomes negotiable. And once identity becomes negotiable, a person can be guided by shame, fear, comparison, or the need to prove themselves.

Many people are not living beneath their calling because they are lazy. They are living beneath their calling because they have been mislabeled, and that label has been feeding quiet agreements for years.

The Woman Reduced to Her Worst Moment
One of the clearest pictures of labeling in Scripture is found in John 8. A woman is dragged into public humiliation because she was caught in adultery. The crowd does not introduce her with compassion. They

do not ask what led her there. They do not consider the possibility of coercion, pain, loneliness, or manipulation. They do not even call her by her name. They present her as a case, a scandal, and a sentence. *"Master, this woman was taken in adultery, in the very act."* ***John 8:4***

Notice what happened to her identity. She was no longer "a woman." She was "the woman caught." She was reduced to a moment, and that moment became a permanent definition, at least in their minds. This is what labels do. They freeze a person in the worst chapter of their story and act as if it is the whole book.

But Jesus does not relate to her through their label. He does not deny her need for change, yet He refuses their condemnation. He exposes the hypocrisy of those who are eager to label others while hiding their own brokenness. *"He that is without sin among you, let him first cast a stone at her."* ***John 8:7***

The stones drop, not because people suddenly became kind, but because truth confronted pride. And when pride is confronted, labels lose their courtroom power.

Then Jesus speaks words that restore identity and responsibility at the same time: *"Neither do I condemn thee: go, and sin no more."* ***John 8:11***

He does not call her what they called her. He releases her from condemnation and calls her forward into a new life. That is what truth does. It does not excuse. It restores. It does not crush. It redirects.

Rahab: When Faith Breaks the Label
Rahab's story challenges every reader who thinks their label is final. Rahab was publicly known by a reputation that carried shame. Scripture does not hide the label people associated with her life: *"And they went, and came into an harlot's house, named Rahab…"* ***Joshua 2:1***

Yet what is powerful about Rahab is not merely what she was known for; it is what she chose to do when truth reached her house. In a moment when she could have preserved herself through fear, she responded through faith. She protected the spies. She aligned with God's people. She took a risk that did not match her label. And later, Scripture speaks of her again, but this time not as a woman trapped by her past. She becomes an example of faith: *"By faith the harlot Rahab perished not…"* ***Hebrews 11:31***

Her label did not have the final say. Her faith did. Rahab's life is proof that God can interrupt identity distortion. He can lift a person out of what people assume and establish them inside what He ordained. He can take a person known for shame and weave them into a story of redemption and legacy. This is not a small detail. It is a pattern of God.

Why Labels Feel Impossible to Remove
If labels were easy to remove, many people would have laid them down a long time ago. The reason labels cling is because they often become intertwined with survival. A person wears them because, at some point, wearing them felt safer than resisting them.

If you were told you were "not enough," you may have learned to overwork so no one could accuse you again. If you were told you were "too much," you may have learned to shrink so you could remain accepted. If you were labeled "a failure," you may have learned to avoid trying so you could avoid pain.

Labels create coping systems. And coping systems, while understandable, can quietly become cages. That is why the renewal of identity is not only emotional—it is mental, spiritual, and deeply intentional. Scripture describes it as transformation through renewed thinking: *"And be not conformed to this world: but be ye transformed by the renewing of your mind..."* **Romans 12:2**

Renewal is not denial. Renewal is a decision to stop allowing the old voice to be the loudest voice.

The Question That Breaks the Agreement
This chapter is not written to accuse you. It is written to bring you back to a place of clarity. Because before a label can fall off, the agreement with it must be identified.

Freedom often begins with one honest question: **Who told you that's who you are?**

Who told you that you are hard to love? Who told you that you always ruin things? Who told you that your past disqualifies your future? Who told you that your weakness is your identity? Who told you that God's grace can reach others, but not you?

Not every voice that spoke into your life had authority. Not every interpretation of your pain was truth. Not every season you survived had permission to rename you. Pain may be real, but pain is not God. Experience may be strong, but experience is not Lord. A label may be loud, but loud is not the same as true.

Reflection
As you sit with this chapter, do not rush to correct yourself or defend your story. Simply begin by noticing. Identify the first time you remember feeling reduced—when a word, an event, or a pattern started shaping how you saw yourself. Pay attention to the labels you repeat silently, especially in moments of pressure, rejection, or fear.

Awareness is not condemnation. Awareness is light. And when light enters, you begin to see what was placed on you versus what belongs to you. You begin to separate who you are from what happened. You begin to recognize that the label may have been part of your story, but it does not have to remain part of your identity. And the journey forward begins the way freedom often begins—quietly, honestly, and courageously with one question:

Who told you that's who you are?

CHAPTER TWO
How Labels Are Formed

Labels Are Not Born; They Are Learned

Labels are rarely formed in a single moment. They are built gradually, layered through words, experiences, reactions, and repetition. Most people cannot pinpoint the exact day a label took root, because it often arrived quietly, without ceremony, and without resistance.

A label begins as an explanation. It then becomes an expectation. Eventually, it settles into identity.

What makes labels powerful is not their accuracy, but their consistency. When the same message is repeated directly or indirectly the mind begins to accept it as truth. Over time, the heart stops questioning it, and the soul starts organizing life around it. This is why two people can experience similar pain and emerge with different identities. One questions the meaning of what happened. The other internalizes it. The difference is not strength; it is interpretation.

The Power of Words Spoken Over Time

Words carry more weight than we often realize, especially when spoken by those with influence. Parents, caregivers, teachers, leaders, and peers all shape identity not only by what they say, but by what they consistently imply.

A child who repeatedly hears "Why can't you ever do anything right?" may eventually stop hearing correction and start hearing definition. A child who grows up in silence may conclude he are invisible. A child praised only for performance may learn that love must be earned. Scripture reminds us of the creative and destructive power of words: *"Death and life are in the power of the tongue."* **Proverbs 18:21**

Words do not simply communicate emotion; they plant seeds. Over time, those seeds grow into beliefs, and beliefs shape identity. Labels often form not because someone intended harm, but because repetition gave a message authority it was never meant to have.

When Pain Explains What Words Did Not Say
Not all labels are spoken. Some are formed through experience alone. Trauma has a way of creating meaning when words are absent. When something painful happens repeatedly and without explanation, the human heart looks inward to make sense of it.

Abandonment can whisper, *You are not worth staying for.* Betrayal can suggest, *You cannot trust anyone.* Abuse can distort identity into shame, even when the victim is innocent.

Pain asks questions, and labels often arrive as answers. This is why people who have endured trauma often carry labels they never consciously chose. Survival required explanation, and the explanation became internalized. Over time, what began as a coping mechanism quietly became identity. Scripture acknowledges this internal struggle: *"The heart knoweth his own bitterness…"* **Proverbs 14:10**

Unprocessed pain rarely remains silent. It speaks sometimes through behavior, sometimes through belief, and often through identity.

Hagar: Labeled, Forgotten, Yet Seen by God
Hagar's story reveals how labels can form through mistreatment and displacement. She was a servant, a foreigner, and a woman without power. When conflict arose, she was dismissed and sent away pregnant, alone, and unseen. From a human perspective, her label was clear: disposable.

Yet something extraordinary happens in her wilderness moment. God does not ignore her pain. He meets her there. Scripture records: *"And the angel of the Lord found her by a fountain of water in the wilderness…"* **Genesis 16:7**

Hagar is the first person in Scripture to name God: *"Thou God seest me."* **Genesis 16:13**

While people labeled her expendable, God identified her as seen. While others dismissed her worth, God acknowledged her presence.

Hagar's story reminds us that labels formed through rejection are not always corrected immediately—but they are never unseen by God. Identity restoration often begins with the simple realization: *I was seen, even when I felt forgotten.*

Repetition Turns Labels into Agreements
One of the most dangerous stages of labeling is when repetition turns belief into agreement. An agreement forms when a person stops questioning a thought and begins organizing their life around it.

"I always mess things up." "This is just how I am." "Nothing good lasts for me."

These statements feel harmless, even honest. But they function as contracts the heart signs with limitation. Scripture warns against this internal alignment with falsehood: *"Casting down imaginations, and every high thing that exalteth itself against the knowledge of God..."* **2 Corinthians 10:5**

A label becomes dangerous when it is no longer examined. Once agreement is made, identity narrows, and potential quietly contracts.

Jacob: When a Name Shapes a Life
Jacob's very name means "supplanter" or "deceiver," and for much of his life, he lived in alignment with it. His actions reflected the meaning placed upon him. He manipulated, struggled, and wrestled for position, as if proving the name assigned to him at birth. Yet God does not leave him there.

In a defining encounter, Jacob wrestles not just with an angel, but with identity itself. And in that moment, God asks a question that mirrors the heart of this book: *"What is thy name?"* **Genesis 32:27**

The question was not for information. It was for confrontation.

God then does what only He can do - He renames him: *"Thy name shall be called no more Jacob, but Israel…"* **Genesis 32:28**

The label that once defined Jacob's struggle no longer had authority over his future. God did not erase Jacob's past, but He redefined Jacob's identity. This is the pattern of redemption.

Why Awareness Is the First Step to Freedom
Labels cannot be removed if they are never identified. Many people pray for freedom while still agreeing with the very beliefs that bind them. Healing does not begin with denial—it begins with awareness. Scripture describes this internal awakening clearly: *"Then ye shall know the truth, and the truth shall make you free."* **John 8:32**

Truth does not rush. It reveals. And revelation creates space for change.

Reflection

As you reflect on this chapter, consider not only the labels spoken over you, but the ones formed through experience, repetition, and survival. Notice which beliefs feel automatic, especially in moments of pressure or fear. Ask yourself where they originated and whether they still deserve authority.

You are not weak for adapting to pain. But you are not required to remain defined by what once helped you survive. Labels may explain where you have been, but they do not have the right to determine where you are going. And awareness, gentle, honest awareness, is the beginning of freedom.

CHAPTER THREE
When Labels Are Reinforced by Religion, Culture, and Comparison

When Systems Strengthen the Label

Some labels are not formed in isolation. They are reinforced by systems - religion, culture, family expectations, and social environments that quietly reward conformity and punish difference. These systems do not always intend harm, but when truth is replaced with performance or comparison, identity becomes fragile.

Religion, when misapplied, can reduce people to their behavior instead of revealing them through grace. Culture can assign value based on appearance, success, gender, age, or status. Comparison convinces people that who they are is insufficient simply because someone else appears to be more.

Labels gain strength when they are affirmed by what surrounds us. A person may leave an abusive home, only to enter a religious environment that reinforces shame. Another may escape poverty only to be labeled "behind" in spaces that worship achievement. Over time, these reinforcements make the label feel validated—no longer personal, but universal.

When Religion Shifts from Healing to Measuring

Faith was never meant to measure people. It was meant to restore them. Yet when spiritual spaces become places of performance rather than transformation, labels multiply. People begin to be known more for what they struggle with than for who they are becoming. Grace becomes conditional. Growth becomes rushed. Pain becomes inconvenient. Jesus addressed this distortion directly: *"They bind heavy burdens and grievous to be borne, and lay them on men's shoulders; but they themselves will not move them with one of their fingers."* **Matthew 23:4**

When faith is reduced to rules without relationship, people learn to hide rather than heal. They learn to present an acceptable version of themselves while carrying unspoken shame beneath the surface. Labels such as "weak," "backslidden," or "not spiritual enough" begin to define identity instead of directing people toward restoration.

The Pharisees: Correct in Doctrine, Blind in Identity

The Pharisees were experts in religious law, yet deeply disconnected from the heart of God. Their commitment to outward righteousness made them harsh toward others and blind toward themselves. They labeled people quickly. Sinners were dismissed. The broken were avoided. The wounded were judged.

Jesus confronted this spirit not because He opposed holiness, but because He opposed hypocrisy disguised as authority. *"Woe unto you, scribes and Pharisees, hypocrites! for ye shut up the kingdom of heaven against men…"* **Matthew 23:13**

Whenever religion shuts people out instead of drawing them in, it has stopped reflecting God's heart and started reinforcing labels.

Culture and the Quiet Pressure to Perform
Culture also plays a powerful role in shaping identity. It assigns value through success, beauty, productivity, independence, and visibility. People learn early what is celebrated and what is ignored. Those who do not fit the cultural mold may internalize labels such as "behind," "inadequate," or "irrelevant." Those who succeed may feel constant pressure to maintain an image they fear losing.

Culture does not ask who you are; it asks what you produce. Scripture cautions against conforming to these pressures: *"Be not conformed to this world…"* **Romans 12:2**

Conformity is subtle. It does not always demand rebellion—it simply demands adjustment. And over time, those adjustments shape identity.

Comparison: The Thief That Looks Harmless
Comparison is one of the most socially accepted forms of identity distortion. It often masquerades as motivation, but its long-term effect is erosion. When a person measures themselves against others, they stop discovering who they are and start managing who they appear to be.

Comparison does not ask, *What am I called to do?* It asks, *Why am I not like them?* Scripture warns of this trap: *"For they measuring themselves by themselves, and comparing themselves among themselves, are not wise."* **2 Corinthians 10:12**

Comparison blinds people to their own grace. It creates unnecessary competition, quiet envy, and persistent dissatisfaction. It reinforces the belief that identity must be earned rather than received.

Mary and Martha: When Comparison Distorts Worth

Mary and Martha both loved Jesus, yet comparison created tension between them. Martha measured faith through activity. Mary measured faith through presence. One felt productive; the other felt devoted. When Martha compared her service to Mary's posture, frustration followed: *"Lord, dost thou not care that my sister hath left me to serve alone?"* **Luke 10:40**

Jesus did not rebuke Martha's service, but He corrected the comparison: *"Martha, Martha, thou art careful and troubled about many things: but one thing is needful..."* **Luke 10:41–42**

Comparison had convinced Martha that her value was tied to performance. Jesus redirected her back to relationship. This is what truth does. It restores balance without dismissing effort.

When Labels Feel Spiritually Justified
One of the most painful distortions occurs when labels are given spiritual language. When someone is told their suffering is a sign of weak faith, or their struggle is evidence of disobedience, shame deepens under the guise of righteousness. Yet Scripture reveals a different posture: *"A bruised reed shall he not break, and smoking flax shall he not quench."* **Isaiah 42:3**

God does not crush what is already wounded. He restores it. Labels that lack compassion do not reflect God's character. They reflect human discomfort with pain.

Reflection
As you reflect on this chapter, consider where external systems may have reinforced internal labels. Notice whether religion, culture, or comparison has influenced how you see yourself more than truth has. Pay attention to moments where you felt pressured to perform, hide, or compete in order to belong.

Truth does not demand comparison. Grace does not require performance. Identity does not need permission from culture.

You were never meant to become a version of yourself that fits someone else's expectation. You were meant to become who you were created to be. And that journey begins when you stop measuring yourself by voices that were never assigned to define you.

CHAPTER FOUR
Living Under a Label You Did Not Choose

When Identity Is Shaped Without Consent
There is a quiet grief that comes from living under a label you never chose. It is the grief of adjustment, the slow reshaping of self to accommodate an identity formed without permission. Many people do not wake up one day and decide who they will become. They adapt. They respond. They adjust to what life demands of them.

A label imposed early often becomes invisible with time. It no longer feels imposed; it feels assumed. The person stops asking whether it is true and starts asking how to survive with it. Life becomes less about discovery and more about management. This is how people learn to live smaller than they were created to be—without ever realizing they made that choice.

The Subtle Cost of Adaptation
Adaptation is not weakness. It is often wisdom in seasons where survival is required. But adaptation becomes costly when it is mistaken for identity. What once helped you endure can later hinder your growth. A child who learned silence to avoid conflict may grow into an adult who struggles to speak their needs. A person who learned perfection to avoid rejection may become exhausted by unrealistic standards. Someone who learned independence to survive abandonment may struggle to receive help even when it is safe.

These patterns are not failures of character. They are responses to environments that did not provide what was needed. Yet when left unexamined, they quietly shape identity and reinforce labels such as *strong but distant, capable but unseen, faithful but tired.* Scripture reminds us that endurance without truth can become bondage: *"Stand fast therefore in the liberty wherewith Christ hath made us free, and be not entangled again with the yoke of bondage."* **Galatians 5:1**

Freedom is not merely escaping pain; it is refusing to remain shaped by it.

Moses: Labeled by Fear Before He Was Called by God
Moses lived under multiple labels before stepping into his calling. Born a Hebrew under threat of death, raised in an Egyptian palace, and later identified as a fugitive after killing an Egyptian, Moses carried a complex and conflicted identity.

By the time God speaks to him from the burning bush, Moses does not introduce himself with confidence. He introduces himself with limitation. *"Who am I, that I should go unto Pharaoh...?"* **Exodus 3:11**

Later, he adds another label: *"O my Lord, I am not eloquent... but I am slow of speech, and of a slow tongue."* **Exodus 4:10**

Moses had learned to define himself by what he lacked rather than by what God had placed within him. His hesitation was not rebellion—it was the result of living under an identity shaped by fear, failure, and years of hiding. Yet God does not debate Moses' label. He replaces it with presence: *"Certainly I will be with thee."* **Exodus 3:12**

Identity restoration often begins not with self-confidence, but with divine assurance.

When the Label Becomes a Boundary

Labels do more than describe, they limit. Once a label is accepted, it begins to function like a boundary, defining what feels permissible and what feels impossible.

A person labeled "unlovable" may reject healthy love because it feels unfamiliar. A person labeled "unstable" may avoid responsibility, fearing failure. A person labeled "strong" may feel unable to rest or ask for help. These boundaries feel protective, but they are often prisons. They keep people from stepping into growth because growth threatens the familiarity of the label. Scripture speaks to this internal captivity: *"For the weapons of our warfare are not carnal, but mighty through God to the pulling down of strong holds."* **2 Corinthians 10:4**

Strongholds are not always sinful behaviors. Often, they are deeply held beliefs about who we are allowed to be.

Gideon: Called While Still Hiding
Gideon's story reveals how labels can coexist with calling—until truth interrupts them. Gideon is found hiding in fear, threshing wheat in secret, trying to survive in a hostile environment. His behavior reflects his identity: cautious, concealed, unsure. Yet when the angel of the Lord appears, Gideon is addressed in a way that contradicts everything he believes about himself: *"The Lord is with thee, thou mighty man of valour."* **Judges 6:12**

Gideon does not accept this immediately. He argues with it. He lists his limitations. He points to his family's insignificance and his own position within it. *"My family is poor in Manasseh, and I am the least in my father's house."* **Judges 6:15**

Gideon's response reveals the power of labels formed through environment and experience. Yet God does not withdraw the calling because of Gideon's self-doubt. He patiently leads him into alignment with truth. Calling often precedes confidence. Truth often speaks before belief catches up.

The Fear of Living Without the Label
One of the reasons labels persist is fear. Fear of who we will be without them. When a label has guided decisions for years, removing it can feel destabilizing.

The question becomes not only, *Who am I?* but, *Who will I be without this explanation?* Without the label:
- Who am I if I am no longer the strong one?
- Who am I if I am no longer the broken one?
- Who am I if I am no longer defined by what happened to me?

This fear is understandable. But Scripture reminds us that identity was never meant to be constructed in isolation: *"It is God which worketh in you both to will and to do of his good pleasure."* **Philippians 2:13**

Identity is not self-invented. It is discovered in relationship with truth.

Reflection
Living under a label you did not choose does not mean you failed. It means you adapted. But adaptation is not destiny. What once protected you does not have to continue defining you.

As you reflect on this chapter, consider the ways you may have adjusted yourself to fit an identity shaped by circumstance rather than truth. Notice where fear has drawn boundaries that no longer serve you. Ask yourself not who you have been, but who you have been becoming beneath the label.

You were never meant to live constrained by a name you did not choose. And freedom does not require you to erase your past—only to release its authority over your future.

CHAPTER FIVE
Breaking the Agreement With the Label

Freedom Begins Where Agreement Ends
Labels gain power not only because they are spoken, but because they are accepted. There is a critical difference between hearing a lie and agreeing with it. Many people did not choose the words that named them, but at some point often unconsciously they learned to live as if those words were true.

Agreement is subtle. It does not always sound like surrender. Sometimes it sounds like realism: "This is just how I am." "I've always been like this." "It's better not to expect too much." "I know my limits."

What feels like honesty is often resignation. And resignation, when left unchallenged, becomes alignment.

Breaking agreement does not mean denying what happened to you. It means refusing to let what happened to you have final authority over who you are becoming.

The Inner Yes That Sustains the Label
Every label survives on an inner yes. That yes may not be spoken aloud, but it is reinforced through thought patterns, emotional reactions, and repeated choices. Over time, the label becomes familiar, and familiarity often feels safer than truth that demands change.

A person may say they want freedom, yet resist opportunities that require them to live differently. Another may pray for healing, yet continue rehearsing beliefs that confirm the label. This is not hypocrisy; it is fear of the unknown. Scripture speaks directly to this inner alignment: *"Neither give place to the devil."* **Ephesians 4:27**

The word *place* implies permission. Labels occupy space in the mind and heart only when room is given to them. Breaking agreement begins when that space is reclaimed.

Why Letting Go Feels Like Losing Control
For many, the label has functioned as an explanation. It has answered painful questions when no better answers were available. Removing it can feel like removing the only structure holding things together.

If I am not "the strong one," who will I be? If I am not "the broken one," how will I explain my pain? If I am not "the problem," what will I do with my anger? Labels can feel stabilizing because they reduce complexity. But stability built on distortion is fragile. It limits growth and keeps the heart locked in patterns that no longer serve it. Scripture invites a different kind of surrender: *"Trust in the Lord with all thine heart; and lean not unto thine own understanding."* **Proverbs 3:5**

Breaking agreement requires trust, trust that truth will hold you even when the old explanation is removed.

Peter: When a Label Is Spoken by Jesus Himself
Peter's story shows that even labels spoken with insight can require transformation. Jesus once says to Peter: *"Thou art Peter, and upon this rock I will build my church."* **Matthew 16:18**

Yet only a short time later, Peter denies Jesus publicly. Fear exposes a fracture between calling and belief. Peter's failure threatens to redefine him, not just in his own eyes, but in the eyes of others.

After the resurrection, Jesus does not confront Peter with accusation. He does not rehearse the failure. Instead, He asks a question three times: *"Lovest thou me?"* **John 21:15–17**

Each question dismantles the agreement Peter might have made with shame. Jesus restores him not by ignoring the failure, but by re-centering his identity in love and purpose. Peter is not defined by denial. He is re-established through relationship. This is how God breaks agreements—with patience, truth, and restoration.

Replacing the Label Requires More Than Awareness
Awareness is the first step, but it is not the final one. Breaking agreement requires replacement. The mind does not remain empty for long. If a false belief is removed without truth taking its place, the old pattern

often returns. Scripture emphasizes this exchange: *"Be renewed in the spirit of your mind."* **Ephesians 4:23**

Renewal is active. It involves intentional reflection, honest questioning, and repeated alignment with truth—even when feelings resist it. This is not a momentary decision. It is a practiced one.

When Truth Feels Unfamiliar
One of the clearest signs that a label is breaking is discomfort. Truth often feels unfamiliar at first. It challenges long-standing narratives and requires new responses. A person who believed they were unworthy may feel uneasy receiving kindness. A person who believed they were weak may feel exposed when stepping into responsibility. A person who believed they were invisible may feel vulnerable being seen. This discomfort is not evidence that truth is wrong. It is evidence that agreement is shifting. Scripture assures us: *"If any man be in Christ, he is a new creature: old things are passed away; behold, all things are become new."* **2 Corinthians 5:17**

Newness does not feel natural at first. It must be learned.

The Courage to Say No Internally
Breaking agreement often begins with a quiet, internal no. Not shouted. Not dramatic. Simply consistent. No, I will not speak to myself that way anymore. No, I will not reduce myself to that moment. No, I will not let this label decide what I attempt. This no does

not deny responsibility. It denies false authority. Scripture calls this resistance: *"Submit yourselves therefore to God. Resist the devil, and he will flee from you."* **James 4:7**

Resistance is not aggression. It is alignment with truth.

Reflection
As you reflect on this chapter, notice where agreement may still exist beneath awareness. Pay attention to the thoughts you excuse as realism and the patterns you protect as normal. Ask yourself which beliefs no longer deserve authority over your choices.

Breaking agreement does not require perfection. It requires consistency. It requires courage to replace what is familiar with what is true. You are not required to carry a label simply because you once needed it to survive. Survival is not the same as identity. And freedom begins, not when the label disappears—but when agreement with it ends.

CHAPTER SIX
Who You Are Beneath the Label

Identity Exists Before the Label Falls Away

One of the quiet fears many people carry is this: *If the label is removed, what will be left?* After years of living beneath a name that explained behavior, pain, and limitation, the idea of identity without it can feel unsettling. Yet identity does not begin when a label is removed. It existed long before the label was ever applied. You are not empty beneath the label. You are not undefined. You are not waiting to be invented. The label covered something real. It did not create it. Scripture affirms that identity precedes experience: *"Before I formed thee in the belly I knew thee..."* **Jeremiah 1:5**

This means your essence was established before words were spoken, before wounds were inflicted, and before conclusions were drawn. What was placed on you never replaced what was placed within you.

The False Fear of Becoming Nothing

Many people resist releasing a label because they confuse it with personality or purpose. The label may have shaped how they survived, how they related, and how they understood themselves. Letting it go can feel like stepping into uncertainty. If I am no longer "the strong one," will I still matter? If I am no longer "the broken one," will anyone understand me? If I am no longer defined by pain, will I lose my story? These fears are understandable. But Scripture reveals a deeper truth: *"In him we live, and move, and have our being."* **Acts 17:28**

Your being is not sustained by labels. It is sustained by God. Identity is not erased when distortion is removed; it is revealed.

David: Anointed Before He Was Acknowledged
David's life reminds us that identity can exist long before recognition. While his brothers were considered strong and impressive, David was overlooked entirely. He was not invited into the room when Samuel came to anoint a king. When Samuel asked if all the sons were present, the response was telling: *"There remaineth yet the youngest, and, behold, he keepeth the sheep."* **1 Samuel 16:11**

David's label was not king. It was insignificant. Unseen. Peripheral. Yet God did not consult the label when choosing him. He bypassed appearance, order, and assumption. *"Man looketh on the outward appearance, but the Lord looketh on the heart."* **1 Samuel 16:7**

David was anointed before he was affirmed. His identity was established before his environment aligned with it. This is often how God works.

What Remains When the Label Is Challenged
When a label is questioned, certain qualities begin to surface—qualities that were always present but muted by fear, shame, or survival. Compassion emerges

where hardness once protected. Courage surfaces where withdrawal once felt safer. Creativity reappears where self-doubt once suppressed expression. These qualities are not new. They are uncovered. Scripture speaks of this unveiling: *"But we all, with open face beholding as in a glass the glory of the Lord, are changed…"*
2 Corinthians 3:18

Change does not always come through force. Often, it comes through recognition.

When Truth Feels Like Exposure
Discovering who you are beneath the label can feel vulnerable. Labels, though limiting, often feel predictable. Truth requires presence. It invites responsibility. It asks you to live from a place of authenticity rather than defense. A person who releases the label of invisibility may have to practice being seen. A person who releases the label of failure may have to risk trying again. A person who releases the label of weakness may have to learn trust. This exposure is not punishment. It is participation. Scripture reassures us: *"For God hath not given us the spirit of fear; but of power, and of love, and of a sound mind."*
2 Timothy 1:7

Fear says exposure will destroy you. Truth says exposure will refine you.

Jesus and the Question of Identity
Throughout His ministry, Jesus consistently redirected people away from labels and toward

identity. He did not relate to individuals according to reputation, status, or history. He addressed fishermen, tax collectors, outcasts, and sinners as people capable of transformation. When Jesus asked His disciples: *"Whom do men say that I am?"* **(Matthew 16:13)** He was not seeking information. He was drawing a distinction between public perception and truth. Identity is not determined by consensus. It is revealed through relationship.

Learning to Live From the Inside Out
Living beneath a label teaches people to manage appearances. Living from identity teaches people to steward truth. The shift is subtle but profound. Instead of asking, *How do I avoid being seen as this?* You begin asking, *How do I live aligned with who I am?* Scripture describes this inward anchoring: *"The kingdom of God is within you."* **Luke 17:21**

Identity work is internal before it is visible. It is cultivated privately before it is expressed publicly.

Reflection
As you reflect on this chapter, consider who you might be beneath the labels you have carried. Notice the qualities that surface when fear loosens its grip. Pay attention to moments when truth feels unfamiliar—not because it is wrong, but because it is new. You are not discovering something foreign. You are returning to something original. The label may have shaped how you lived, but it never owned who you were. And as you continue this journey,

what is beneath the label will become clearer, stronger, and more secure. Identity does not need to be constructed. It needs to be uncovered.

CHAPTER SEVEN
When God Calls You by a Different Name

Names Carry Authority

Throughout Scripture, names are never casual. They carry meaning, direction, and authority. To name something is to define its nature, its function, and its future. This is why labels are so powerful—and why God is intentional when He renames.

A label spoken by people often reflects limitation. A name spoken by God reflects destiny. Many people live caught between these two voices. One reminds them of who they were. The other calls them into who they are becoming. The struggle is not always about disbelief in God—it is about familiarity with the old name. When God calls you by a different name, He is not ignoring your history. He is announcing your future.

Abram to Abraham: When Promise Interrupts Limitation

Abram's name meant "exalted father," yet his life contradicted it. He was advanced in age and childless. The gap between his name and his experience likely carried quiet disappointment and confusion. Yet God does not wait for circumstances to change before He speaks identity. Scripture records: *"Neither shall thy name any more be called Abram, but thy name shall be Abraham; for a father of many nations have I made thee."*
Genesis 17:5

Notice the tense. *Have I made thee.* God speaks as though the future is already established. The renaming did not immediately change Abraham's situation, but it changed the authority governing his identity. God was teaching Abraham to live from promise rather than appearance. This is often how transformation begins—not with evidence, but with alignment.

Why God Renames Before We Are Ready
God often speaks identity before we feel qualified to carry it. This is not because He is unaware of our weaknesses, but because He is unwilling to let weakness have the final word. If identity were based on readiness, no one would ever be called forward. Scripture confirms this divine pattern: *"But God hath chosen the foolish things of the world to confound the wise; and God hath chosen the weak things of the world to confound the things which are mighty."* **1 Corinthians 1:27**

When God renames, He is not flattering. He is establishing truth.

Simon to Peter: When Instability Meets Calling
Simon's name reflected his nature—impulsive, emotional, inconsistent. Yet Jesus saw beyond the behavior and addressed the foundation beneath it. *"And I say also unto thee, That thou art Peter, and upon this rock I will build my church."* **Matthew 16:18**

Peter would still struggle. He would still fail. But the name spoken by Jesus carried authority greater than Peter's inconsistency.

Peter's journey shows us something critical: God does not rename people because they are already stable. He renames them because stability is part of what He is producing. The label says, *This is what you are now.* God's name says, *This is who you are becoming.*

When the Old Name Tries to Follow You
Even after God speaks a new name, the old one often tries to linger. People may continue to treat you according to who you were. Your own thoughts may revert under pressure. Old environments may reinforce familiar identities. This tension is not a sign that God's word failed. It is a sign that transition is taking place. Scripture addresses this inner conflict: *"For the flesh lusteth against the Spirit, and the Spirit against the flesh…"* **Galatians 5:17**

The struggle is not between good and evil—it is between old alignment and new truth.

Saul to Paul: When Purpose Redefines Identity
Saul's identity was deeply rooted in reputation, authority, and religious performance. His name carried weight, influence, and fear. Yet when he encountered Jesus, everything he had built his identity upon collapsed. Scripture records: *"Saul, Saul, why persecutest thou me?"* **Acts 9:4**

The encounter did not simply correct behavior—it dismantled identity. Saul's transformation into Paul represented a shift from self-constructed authority to God-defined purpose. Paul's new name reflected a new posture: humility, dependence, and mission. God was not improving Saul. He was reorienting him.

Learning to Answer to the New Name
One of the most practical challenges in identity restoration is learning to respond to the name God speaks, even when it feels unfamiliar. This requires intentional alignment—choosing to agree with truth over habit. You answer to the new name when:
- You make decisions based on truth rather than fear.
- You receive grace instead of resisting it.
- You stop rehearsing the old story as justification.
- You allow growth without self-sabotage.

Scripture encourages this posture: *"Put on the new man, which after God is created in righteousness and true holiness."* **Ephesians 4:24**

Putting on the new does not happen once. It is practiced.

When God's Name Conflicts With Your Feelings
Feelings are powerful, but they are not authoritative. Often, God's name for you will contradict how you feel about yourself—especially in seasons of healing. You may feel weak while God calls you strong. You may feel unseen while God calls you chosen. You may feel unworthy while God calls you beloved. Scripture affirms this tension: *"Let God be true, but every man a liar."* **Romans 3:4**

Truth does not wait for agreement to remain true. It stands.

Reflection
As you reflect on this chapter, consider the names God has spoken over people throughout Scripture—names that contradicted circumstance, history, and feeling. Consider the possibility that God has been calling you by a name you have not yet learned to answer to. Pay attention to which names you respond to most easily—the ones shaped by fear or the ones shaped by promise. Notice where the old name still tries to assert authority, and where truth is quietly inviting alignment. You are not required to earn the name God gives you. You are invited to grow into it. And as this journey continues, the voice that once defined you will grow quieter—while the voice that created you becomes clearer.

CHAPTER EIGHT
Healing the Wounds That Gave the Label Power

Labels Draw Strength From Unhealed Pain

Labels do not gain their deepest power from words alone. They gain power from wounds that were never addressed. A label spoken over a healed heart often falls flat. A label spoken into an open wound, however, can take root and remain for years. Pain gives labels credibility.

When hurt is unresolved, the heart searches for meaning. It asks questions such as, *Why did this happen? What does this say about me? What should I expect from life now?* Labels often arrive disguised as answers to those questions. They may not be true, but they feel explanatory and that makes them persuasive. Healing, therefore, is not optional to identity restoration. Without healing, labels remain emotionally reinforced even after they are intellectually rejected.

Why Avoided Pain Continues to Speak

Many people believe time heals wounds. In reality, time only covers what truth does not touch. Pain that is avoided does not disappear, it adapts. It shows up as defensiveness, withdrawal, anger, self-doubt, perfectionism, or numbness. These responses are not flaws. They are evidence of wounds trying to protect themselves. Scripture acknowledges the lasting effect of untreated pain: *"Hope deferred maketh the heart sick…"* **Proverbs 13:12**

A sick heart is not a sinful heart. It is a wounded one. And wounds require care, not condemnation.

The Difference Between Remembering and Reliving

Healing does not require forgetting what happened. It requires changing how what happened continues to speak. Many people relive pain without realizing it, rehearsing moments, replaying words, and reinforcing beliefs formed in trauma. Reliving keeps the wound open. Remembering allows it to be addressed. Scripture offers wisdom on this distinction: *"Forgetting those things which are behind, and reaching forth unto those things which are before…"* **Philippians 3:13**

This is not about denial. It is about direction. Healing begins when the past is no longer the loudest voice in the present.

The Woman With the Issue of Blood: A Wound Carried for Years

The woman with the issue of blood lived with both a physical condition and a social label. For twelve years, her bleeding defined her experience medically, socially, and spiritually. She was considered unclean, isolated, and untouchable. Scripture tells us: *"And a certain woman, which had an issue of blood twelve years…"* **Mark 5:25**

Her wound shaped her identity. It determined where she could go, who she could touch, and how she was perceived. Yet her healing did not begin with public validation. It began with a private decision to reach for truth. *"If I may touch but his clothes, I shall be whole."* **Mark 5:28**

Jesus does not heal her anonymously. He calls her forward and names her differently: *"Daughter, thy faith hath made thee whole…"* **Mark 5:34**

Notice the shift. She is no longer identified by her wound. She is identified by relationship. Healing did not just stop the bleeding, it restored her identity.

Why Healing Often Feels Slower Than Deliverance

Some wounds are healed instantly. Others heal gradually. This does not reflect the depth of faith; it reflects the complexity of the wound. Trauma, betrayal, and prolonged pain often require layered healing. Scripture confirms this patient process: *"He healeth the broken in heart, and bindeth up their wounds."* **Psalm 147:3**

Binding a wound is intentional. It is careful. It is protective. God does not rush what requires gentleness. Healing is not dramatic for everyone. Sometimes it looks like:
- Feeling without being overwhelmed
- Remembering without collapsing
- Speaking without fear
- Trusting without losing yourself

These are signs of restoration.

When Healing Threatens the Label
One reason healing is resisted is because it threatens the label. If the wound heals, the explanation disappears. The identity shaped around pain must be reexamined.

Who am I if I am no longer the abandoned one? Who am I if I am no longer the rejected one? Who am I if I am no longer defined by what hurt me? This fear is understandable. But Scripture offers reassurance: *"The Lord is nigh unto them that are of a broken heart..."* **Psalm 34:18**

God does not abandon people when they let go of pain. He draws nearer.

Healing Reclaims Authority From the Past
Unhealed wounds keep the past in authority. Healed wounds return authority to the present. This shift is subtle but profound. When healing occurs, reactions soften, choices expand, and identity stabilizes. Scripture speaks to this restoration of authority: *"For God hath not given us the spirit of fear; but of power, and of love, and of a sound mind."* **2 Timothy 1:7**

A sound mind is not the absence of memory. It is the absence of control by memory.

Reflection

As you reflect on this chapter, consider which wounds may still be giving power to old labels. Notice where pain continues to shape reactions, expectations, or beliefs. Be honest, but gentle with yourself. Healing does not demand speed—it invites truth. You are not required to minimize what hurt you in order to heal. But you are invited to release its authority over your identity. When wounds heal, labels lose their voice. When truth restores, the past loosens its grip. And what remains is not weakness—but clarity.

CHAPTER NINE
Learning to See Yourself Clearly Again

When Distortion Becomes Familiar
After years of living under labels, many people no longer trust their own perception. They do not know whether what they see in themselves is truth, fear, memory, or habit. Distortion becomes familiar, and familiarity often feels safer than clarity.

When a person has been told who they are for a long time, they may stop looking at themselves honestly. They learn to see through the lens of expectation rather than truth. That lens exaggerates weakness, minimizes strength, and filters out anything that contradicts the label. Seeing clearly again requires unlearning before it requires discovery.

The Mirror We Learn to Use
Every person uses a mirror to understand themselves. For some, that mirror is family opinion. For others, it is past failure, comparison, or religious performance. These mirrors do not reflect truth; they reflect interpretation. Scripture introduces a different kind of mirror: *"For if any be a hearer of the word, and not a doer, he is like unto a man beholding his natural face in a glass."* **James 1:23**

This passage is not merely about obedience. It is about reflection. The Word of God functions as a mirror that reveals what is actually present—not what fear, shame, or memory has distorted. Until the mirror changes, perception remains compromised.

Why Clear Vision Feels Uncomfortable at First

Clarity can feel threatening when distortion has been protective. A label, even a painful one, often explains suffering and provides a narrative that makes sense of chaos. Removing distortion requires the courage to look without defense. When a person begins to see themselves clearly:

- Strength may surface where weakness once dominated.
- Responsibility may emerge where blame once lived.
- Possibility may appear where limitation once ruled.

This shift can feel disorienting. Yet Scripture reminds us: *"The light shineth in darkness; and the darkness comprehended it not."* **John 1:5**

Darkness does not resist light because light is wrong. It resists because light reveals.

Blind Bartimaeus: When Vision Is Restored, Identity Changes

Blind Bartimaeus had an identity shaped by limitation. He was known as a beggar, a man defined by what he lacked. When Jesus passed by, Bartimaeus cried out—not for charity, but for sight. Scripture records: *"Jesus, thou Son of David, have mercy on me."* **Mark 10:47**

When Jesus asks what he wants, the request is simple and direct: *"Lord, that I might receive my sight."* **Mark 10:51**

Once his sight is restored, Bartimaeus does not return to begging. Scripture says: *"And immediately he received his sight, and followed Jesus in the way."* **Mark 10:52**

Vision altered his direction. Seeing clearly changed how he lived. This is what clarity does. It does not just improve perception; it reshapes movement.

Separating Observation From Judgment
One of the most important skills in seeing clearly again is learning to observe without condemning. Many people confuse self-awareness with self-judgment. As a result, they avoid reflection altogether. Truth does not accuse. It reveals. Scripture affirms this posture: *"There is therefore now no condemnation to them which are in Christ Jesus…"* **Romans 8:1**

Condemnation clouds vision. Grace clarifies it. When you learn to see yourself without accusation, growth becomes possible. You stop defending and start understanding. You stop hiding and start healing.

When Old Images Try to Resurface
Even after healing begins, old images may resurface under pressure. Stress, conflict, or fatigue can trigger familiar perceptions. This does not mean progress

has been lost. It means a new way of seeing is still being practiced. Scripture acknowledges this process: *"We walk by faith, not by sight."* **2 Corinthians 5:7**

Faith here is not denial of reality; it is commitment to truth when perception wavers. Clear vision is not permanent awareness—it is practiced alignment.

Seeing Yourself as God Sees You
God's perspective is not shaped by your worst moment, your longest struggle, or your loudest failure. It is shaped by truth, intention, and purpose. Scripture expresses this divine clarity: *"The Lord seeth not as man seeth…"* **1 Samuel 16:7**

When you begin to adopt God's view of yourself, the internal dialogue changes. Compassion replaces contempt. Responsibility replaces shame. Growth replaces stagnation. This is not self-exaltation. It is alignment.

Clarity Restores Dignity
One of the quiet gifts of seeing clearly again is dignity. Dignity returns when a person stops relating to themselves as a problem to manage and begins relating to themselves as a person to steward. Dignity does not eliminate humility. It establishes worth. Scripture affirms this restoration: *"Thou hast made him a little lower than the angels, and hast crowned him with glory and honour."* **Psalm 8:5**

When dignity returns, boundaries strengthen, relationships shift, and choices become intentional rather than reactive.

Reflection

As you reflect on this chapter, notice the mirrors you have been using to understand yourself. Ask whether they reflect truth or distortion. Pay attention to moments when clarity feels uncomfortable, and remind yourself that discomfort often accompanies healing. You are not learning to see someone new. You are learning to see yourself without distortion. And as vision returns, so does direction. As clarity grows, so does confidence—not the loud kind, but the steady kind rooted in truth. Seeing clearly again is not a destination. It is a way of living.

CHAPTER TEN
Living Free Without Needing the Label

Freedom Is Not the Absence of Memory
Living free does not mean forgetting what happened to you. It means no longer requiring a label to explain yourself, defend yourself, or justify your limits. Freedom is not amnesia; it is authority restored to the present.

Many people fear freedom because they assume it requires erasing the past. In reality, freedom reframes the past. It allows you to remember without reliving, to acknowledge without being governed, and to move forward without dragging an old identity behind you. Scripture speaks to this release: *"Stand fast therefore in the liberty wherewith Christ hath made us free…"* **Galatians 5:1**

Freedom must be stood in. It is not accidental.

When the Label Is No Longer Needed
There comes a point in healing when the label no longer serves any purpose. It no longer explains your behavior, protects your heart, or organizes your decisions. What once felt necessary begins to feel restrictive. You notice that you no longer introduce yourself through pain. You stop rehearsing your story to justify boundaries. You respond rather than react.

This is not denial. This is integration. The label is no longer needed because identity has stabilized.

Scripture affirms this maturity: *"When I was a child, I spake as a child... but when I became a man, I put away childish things."* **1 Corinthians 13:11**

Letting go is not loss. It is growth.

Freedom Requires Responsibility
Living without a label means you can no longer blame the past for present choices. This responsibility can feel heavy at first, but it is also empowering. When you are no longer governed by what happened, you are free to choose who you will be. Responsibility does not mean perfection. It means ownership. Scripture connects freedom and responsibility clearly: *"For, brethren, ye have been called unto liberty; only use not liberty for an occasion to the flesh..."* **Galatians 5:13**

Freedom is not reckless. It is intentional.

Joseph: Free Before the Circumstances Changed
Joseph's story shows us what internal freedom looks like. Betrayed by his brothers, falsely accused, and imprisoned, Joseph had every reason to live under labels of rejection, injustice, and abandonment. Yet even in confinement, Joseph did not adopt the identity of a victim. He remained faithful, discerning, and aligned with purpose. Scripture records his posture years later: *"Ye thought evil against me; but God meant it unto good..."* **Genesis 50:20**

Joseph did not deny what happened. He refused to live defined by it. This is freedom—when bitterness is no longer needed to explain your story.

Living Without Needing to Be Understood
One of the quiet signs of freedom is the release from the need to be constantly understood. When a label governed your life, you may have felt compelled to explain yourself—to justify reactions, boundaries, or choices. Freedom removes that urgency. Scripture reassures us: *"It is the Lord who judges me."* **1 Corinthians 4:4**

When identity is secure, misunderstanding loses its power. You stop correcting narratives that no longer define you.

The Return of Simplicity
Labels complicate life. They require constant maintenance—defending, hiding, proving, or compensating. Freedom simplifies. Decisions become clearer. Relationships become healthier. Energy once spent managing perception is redirected toward growth and presence. Jesus describes this simplicity: *"My yoke is easy, and my burden is light."* **(Matthew 11:30)** Freedom is not loud. It is light.

When the Old Voice Tries to Return
Old labels may occasionally attempt to resurface, especially during stress or transition. This does not mean freedom has been lost. It means discernment is required. The difference now is awareness. The voice

is recognized and dismissed rather than believed. Scripture encourages this discernment: *"Try the spirits whether they are of God..."* **1 John 4:1**

Freedom is not the absence of challenge. It is the presence of clarity.

Living Forward Without Negotiation
Once a person no longer needs a label, life begins to move forward without negotiation. Choices are made from truth rather than fear. Boundaries are set without guilt. Growth is pursued without self-sabotage. Scripture affirms this forward posture: *"If any man be in Christ, he is a new creature..."* **2 Corinthians 5:17**

Newness does not coexist with old agreements.

Reflection
As you reflect on this chapter, notice where you may still be tempted to explain yourself through an old label. Ask whether that explanation is still necessary—or whether it is simply familiar. Pay attention to moments where freedom feels quiet rather than dramatic, simple rather than intense. You are not required to carry what you have outgrown. You are not obligated to remain who you were when you were wounded. Living free does not mean you have no story. It means your story no longer owns you. And when the label is no longer needed, life opens—not into perfection, but into peace.

FINAL CHAPTER
Who Told You the Truth About You?

The Most Important Voice Was Always the Last One

Throughout this journey, one question has guided every chapter, every reflection, and every unveiling: *Who told you that's who you are?* But there is a second question—one that carries even more weight, because it determines what happens next:

Who Told You the Truth About You?

Labels are loud, but truth is patient. Labels rush to define; truth waits to be discovered. Many people spend their lives reacting to the voices that named them, never pausing long enough to listen for the voice that created them.

The most powerful truth about your identity was never spoken in anger, fear, or disappointment. It was spoken in intention.

Truth Was Present Before the Label Ever Arrived

Before words wounded you, before experiences shaped conclusions, before survival demanded adaptation, truth already existed. Identity was not formed in response to pain—it was established before pain ever entered the story. Scripture reminds us of this origin: *"For we are his workmanship, created in Christ Jesus unto good works…"* **Ephesians 2:10**

This means your identity was not an accident. It was not improvised. It was not shaped by failure or defined by loss. What happened to you may have influenced your journey, but it never authored your worth. Truth was always older than the label.

When Jesus Spoke, Identity Was Restored

Jesus consistently spoke truth over people who had been misnamed. He did not wait for them to correct themselves. He did not demand they earn a new identity. He spoke truth where distortion had ruled. To the woman bent over for eighteen years, He said: *"Woman, thou art loosed from thine infirmity."* **Luke 13:12**

To Zacchaeus, the one known as a sinner and extortioner, He said: *"This day is salvation come to this house…"* **Luke 19:9**

To the disciples - confused, fearful, and inconsistent - He said: *"Ye are the light of the world."* **Matthew 5:14**

Jesus did not speak based on reputation. He spoke based on truth.

Truth Does Not Compete - It Replaces

One of the most freeing realizations is this: truth does not need to argue with a label. It outlasts it. When truth is consistently chosen, the label loses relevance without drama.

You do not have to keep confronting the past once truth becomes your reference point. You stop asking,

Is this who I am? and begin asking, *Is this aligned with truth?* Scripture captures this exchange: *"Sanctify them through thy truth: thy word is truth."* **John 17:17**

Truth sanctifies—it separates what is false from what is real.

Living Answered Instead of Questioning
For much of life, people live questioning themselves. They question their worth, their decisions, their voice, their place, and their belonging. Labels thrive in that uncertainty. Truth brings rest.

When truth settles in the heart, the internal interrogation ends. You no longer live trying to prove who you are or defend who you are not. You begin living answered. Scripture describes this confidence: *"The Spirit itself beareth witness with our spirit, that we are the children of God."* **Romans 8:16**

When truth bears witness, striving fades.

The Quiet Authority of Knowing Who You Are
Knowing who you are does not make you loud. It makes you grounded. It does not make you aggressive. It makes you discerning. You stop negotiating your value and start stewarding your life. This authority shows up quietly:
- In boundaries set without guilt
- In love given without fear
- In correction received without collapse
- In growth pursued without self-betrayal

Scripture reflects this maturity: *"Let your moderation be known unto all men."* **Philippians 4:5**

Truth produces stability, not spectacle.

When the Old Label No Longer Answers You

There may come moments when the old label tries to speak again—through memory, pressure, or fear. But something will be different now. The label will no longer sound convincing. It will no longer feel authoritative. Not because you fought it—but because you outgrew it. Scripture affirms this quiet victory: *"And ye shall know the truth, and the truth shall make you free."* **John 8:32**

Freedom does not announce itself. It settles.

You Were Always More Than the Name You Were Given

If this book has done its work, it has not given you a new identity. It has reminded you of one that was always there. It has helped you remove what was placed on you so that what was placed within you could rise. You are not what happened to you. You are not what was said over you. You are not what you survived. You are what truth has always said you are.

Reflection

As you close this book, you do not need to rush into anything new. Simply notice what feels lighter. Notice what no longer needs defending. Notice what feels steady instead of strained. Truth has a way of making itself known—not through force, but through peace. And if you ever find yourself asking again, *Who am I?* Return to the question that changes everything: **Who told me the truth about me?** Let that voice be the one you answer to.

Prayer
Father,
I thank You for truth—the kind that heals quietly, restores gently, and remains when every other voice fades. I thank You for every reader who has carried a name they did not choose, a burden they did not deserve, and a story that felt heavier than it should have been. Where labels formed through pain, speak truth. Where identity was distorted through words, experiences, or silence, restore clarity. Where survival required adaptation, bring freedom without shame. Heal the places that were wounded in secret. Release the heart from agreements made in fear, confusion, or loneliness. Let every false name lose its authority, and let truth take its rightful place. Teach us to see ourselves as You see us—not through our past, not through our failures, not through what was done to us—but through the purpose You established before time began. May every reader walk forward lighter, steadier, and free—no longer striving to prove who they are, but resting in the truth of who You say they are. In Jesus' name, Amen.

AUTHOR'S NOTE

If you have read this book, it means you are willing to look inward with honesty and courage. That willingness matters more than you may realize. Healing does not begin with certainty—it begins with truth.

This book was written to create space. Space to question what you were told. Space to separate who you are from what happened. Space to release labels that may have explained your pain, but were never meant to define your identity.

If something in these pages feels familiar, heavy, or deeply personal, know that you are not alone. Many carry these stories quietly. Many learn to function while still feeling unseen. My hope is that this book reminds you that identity is not something you must earn or rebuild—it is something you are allowed to recover.

Take what serves you. Leave what does not. Return to these pages whenever the old voice tries to speak again. Truth is patient, and it will meet you every time you choose to listen.

Thank you for trusting this journey.

Prophetess Dr. Racheal Odoy

ABOUT THE AUTHOR

Dr. Racheal Odoy is an author, minister, and speaker committed to helping individuals rediscover truth, identity, and wholeness through faith and reflection. With a compassionate yet insightful voice, she addresses issues of identity distortion, healing, and spiritual restoration, drawing from Scripture and lived experience.

Her work speaks to readers seeking clarity beyond labels, freedom from past wounds, and a deeper understanding of who they are through God's truth. Dr. Odoy writes with depth, grace, and global relevance, creating space for healing without judgment and truth without condemnation.

www.ingramcontent.com/pod-product-compliance
Lightning Source LLC
Chambersburg PA
CBHW050704160426
43194CB00010B/1999